P9-CEI-856

Program Authors

Peter Afflerbach

Camille Blachowicz

Candy Dawson Boyd

Wendy Cheyney

Connie Juel

Edward Kame'enui

Donald Leu

Jeanne Paratore

P. David Pearson

Sam Sebesta

Deborah Simmons

Sharon Vaughn

Susan Watts-Taffe

Karen Kring Wixson

PEARSON

Scott Foresman

Editorial Offices: Glenview, Illinois • Parsippany, New Jersey • New York, New York
Sales Offices: Boston, Massachusetts • Duluth, Georgia • Glenview, Illinois
Coppell, Texas • Sacramento, California • Mesa, Arizona

We dedicate Reading Street to
Peter Jovanovich.

His wisdom, courage,
and passion for education
are an inspiration to us all.

About the Cover Artist

Daniel Moreton lives in New York City, where he uses his computer to create illustrations for books. When he is not working, Daniel enjoys cooking, watching movies, and traveling. On a trip to Mexico, Daniel was inspired by all of the bright colors around him. He likes to use those colors in his art.

ISBN-13: 978-0-328-24344-0
ISBN-10: 0-328-24344-2

2 3 4 5 6 7 8 9 10 V063 16 15 14 13 12 11 10 09 08 07
CC:N1

Dear Reader,

Are you enjoying your travels along *Scott Foresman Reading Street?* What new skills have you learned to help you read and understand new things? What strategies have helped you smooth out the "bumps in the road" as you read?

As you continue along *Scott Foresman Reading Street,* you will read about people in communities at home, in school, and in neighborhoods. You will also read about communities in nature. So, buckle your seat belt and enjoy the trip!

Sincerely,
The Authors

Communities

What is a community?

People in Communities

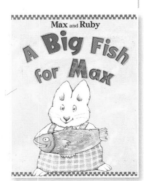

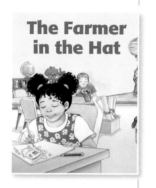

Communities in Nature

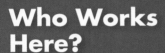

Let's Talk About
People in Communities

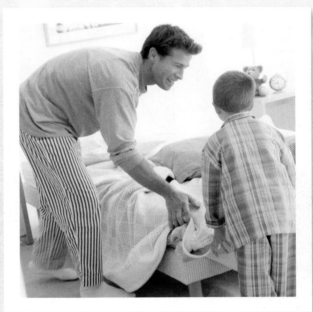

Words to Read

want

good

catch

no

put

Read the Words

1. Max said, "I want a fish."

2. Fish are good to eat.

3. Will Max catch a fish?

4. No fish bit.

5. We put the fish in a pan.

Genre: Animal Fantasy

An animal fantasy is a story with animals that act like humans. Next you will read about Max and Ruby—rabbits that go fishing.

Max and Ruby

A Big Fish for Max

written and designed by
Rosemary Wells

illustrated
by **Jody Wheeler**

Where will Max
get a big fish?

"I wish I had a fish to eat," said Max.

"Then we will catch a big fish,"
said Grandma.

"We can walk to the park," said Ruby.

"And Max will catch a big fish."

"Good," said Max. "Yum, yum, yum!"

The path in the park led to the pond.

"Max can fish in this pond," said Ruby.

Max sat.

He got a red ball in his net.

But no fish bit.

Then Max got a black ship in his net.
But no fish bit.

And then Max got a clam shell
in his net.

"I want to call the fish," said Ruby.
"Then I can talk to the fish."
But still no fish bit.

"Well, we can all walk to the fish
shop," said Grandma.
"And we can talk to the fish man."

The fish man had lots of fish in a box.
"We want a fresh fish," said Grandma.
"That fat fish is good."

At home, Grandma put the fish
in a hot pan.
Then Ruby put the fish in a dish.

"Yum, yum, yum!" said Max.

Think and Share

Talk About It Max, Ruby, and Grandma care about each other. Find and read one part of the story that shows caring.

1. Use the pictures below to retell the story.
Retell

2. What was this story mostly about? **Main Idea**

3. Did you predict that Max would catch a fish? Find the part of the story that shows whether you were right. **Predict**

Look Back and Write Look back at pages 20–22. Max did not catch a fish. What did he catch? Write those things.

Meet the Author
Rosemary Wells

Ms. Wells says, "Some of my most pleasurable memories as a child were of fishing with my father. We used to catch snapper blues, and my mother cooked them in parsley and butter that night. Today fish is still one of my favorite things to eat."

When Rosemary Wells writes stories about Max and Ruby, she thinks about what her own two girls said and did when they were children.

Read other books by Rosemary Wells.

At Home

We all want to help.
This plant is no good.
We dig it up.

Dad puts pots on the shelf.

Mom cuts the grass.

Sis can catch Gus.
We talk and have fun.

Write Now

Writing and Grammar

List

Prompt

In *A Big Fish for Max*, a family goes fishing in the park. Think about things your family does together. Now list sentences about three of these things, starting each sentence with *My family.* . . .

Writing Trait

Choose words that tell about actions.

Student Model

Title tells what list is about.

Each sentence shows a different action.

Writer <u>chooses</u> clear <u>words.</u>

Things My Family Does
Together
My family eats meals.
My family shops at stores.
My family rides bikes.

Grammar

Nouns

A **noun** names a person, a place, an animal, or a thing.

The word **man** names a person.
The word **park** names a place.
The word **fish** names an animal.
The word **net** names a thing.

. . . .

Look at the list. Write the nouns in the title and the sentences.

Let's Talk About

People in Communities

Words to Read

could
be
old
paper
horse

Read the Words

1. Dave could be the pig in the class play.

2. Beth has an old hat for the play.

3. The class made paper masks.

4. Jake made a horse mask.

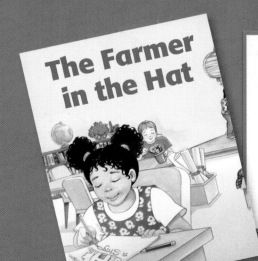

The Farmer in the Hat

Genre: Realistic Fiction
Realistic fiction has characters that act like real people. You will read a story about classmates putting on a play.

The Farmer in the Hat

by Pat Cummings

Beth

Dave

Grace

Who will be the farmer in the play?

Max

Jake

Meg

41

"I have the hat. I could be
the farmer, Old MacDonald,
in this play," said Beth.

"No, I will be the farmer," said Dave.

"You can be a pig," said Beth.
"A pig!" Dave made a face.

43

Grace went up on the stage.
"We could make paper masks,"
she said. "Ducks, hens, a pig,
a horse!"

"I have the hat!" said Max.
"I will be Old MacDonald,
not Beth!"

"Let me have that hat!" Dave said.

"Stop!" said Grace. "We must make masks."

Old MacDonald
★ Hens = Beth and Grace
★ Pig = Dave
★ Duck = Max
★ Farmer = ?

Max made a duck on his page.
Beth made hens.

Dave made a pig mask on his page.

"That is one odd pig," Grace said.

"It takes ages to make this horse mask," said Jake.

"I can make my mask fast," said Meg.

She made a fat gerbil mask.

"Place that gerbil in a paper cage," Jake said with a grin.

"Take your places up on the stage," said Grace.

"Grunt!" Dave had on his pig mask.

"Squeak!" said Meg.

"Quack!" Max had on his duck mask.

"Cluck." Beth had on her hen mask.

"Look at the cat!" said Grace.
"That is one odd farmer!"

Think and Share

Talk About It The author wrote a funny story about a class play. Read your favorite part of the story.

1. Use the pictures below to retell the story.
Retell

2. Why did the children forget about the farmer's hat? Cause/Effect

3. The pictures give a clue about how the story will end. What clues do you see?
Monitor/Fix Up

Look Back and Write Look back at the story. List the animals that will be in the play.

54

Meet the Author and Illustrator
Pat Cummings

Pat Cummings once played a rabbit in a school play, and her sister played a grasshopper. Ms. Cummings made the cat the farmer in this story because "cats seem to naturally find the center of attention."

Ms. Cummings loves writing children's books. "The best part is that I can explore almost any subject."

Read two more books by Pat Cummings.

Helping Hands at 4-H
by Lindy Russell

Where could you see what farmers do? At a 4-H club!

How old are kids in 4-H? They can be ages 8 to 18.

At 4-H you can take care of
a horse or a pig.

You can get the eggs from the hens.

This 4-H club has a bake sale.
They place an ad in the paper.
They sell eggs too.

The sale is good!
The club will get chicks.

The chicks will get big.
Then the club will have lots
of eggs to sell.

Write Now

Writing and Grammar

Invitation

Prompt

In *The Farmer in the Hat,* the children put on a play.
Think about an event your class is planning.
Now write an invitation asking a friend to come to the event.

Writing Trait

An invitation may have some **sentences.**

Student Model

Invitation gives information person needs.

Polite word sounds friendly.

Sentence begins and ends correctly.

From: Emily Martinez

To: Madison Hyde

Please come to my class

art fair.

Date: Friday, May 2, 2008

Time: 10 A.M.

Place: Room 110

62

Grammar

Proper Nouns

Special names for people, places, animals, and things are called **proper nouns.** Proper nouns begin with capital letters.

Max took the hat from **B**eth.

Max and **Beth** are proper nouns. They tell the names of a boy and a girl. **Max** and **Beth** begin with capital letters.

• •

Look at the invitation. Write the proper nouns.

Let's Talk About
People in Communities

Mayor Sterling

65

Words to Read

people
live
work
who
out

Read the Words

1. People live here.

2. People work here too.

3. Who works here?

4. Who puts out fires?

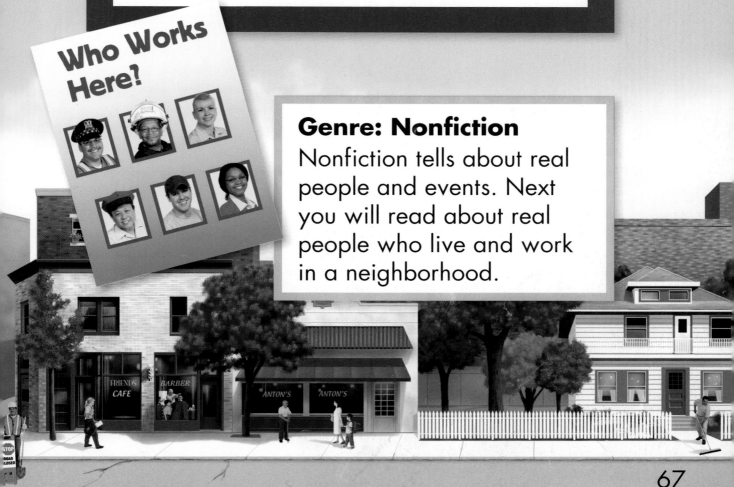

Genre: Nonfiction
Nonfiction tells about real people and events. Next you will read about real people who live and work in a neighborhood.

Who Works

FRIENDS CAFE

BARBER

ANTON'S ANTON'S

STOP ROAD CLOSED

Who works where you live?

Here?

by Melissa Blackwell Burke
illustrated by Tim Spransy

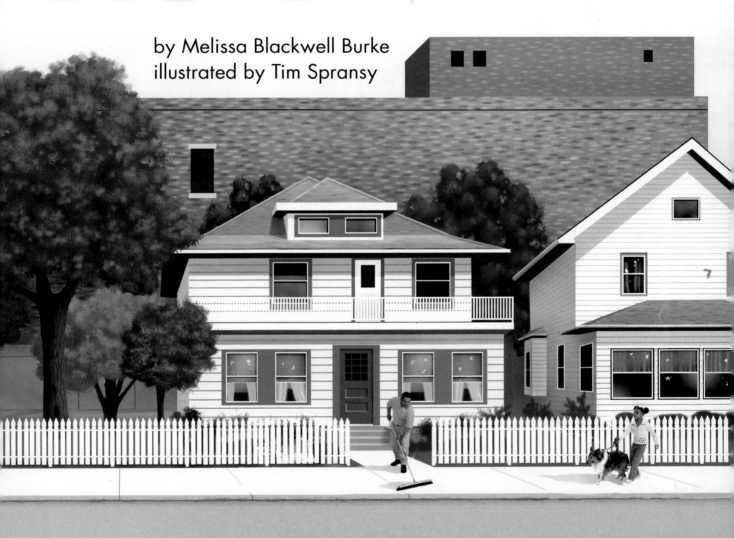

People live and work
in this neighborhood.
It is such a busy place.

Who works in this place?
We will talk to them.
They all like to help us.

I make the neighborhood safe.
When you ride your bike,
stop and check all ways.
I will help you cross.

I help put out fires. Fire can be bad.
I wish all people could be safe
from fire.

I put mail in your box.
People stop and wave and smile.
They like to chat a while.

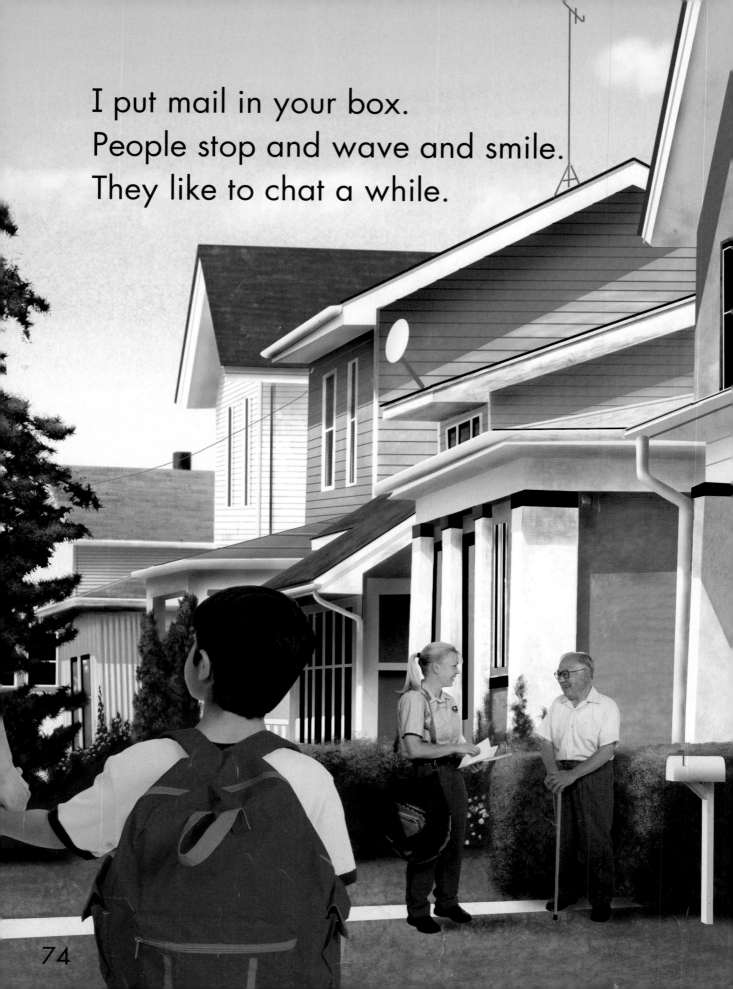

I drive a big bus.
People can ride this bus to work.
I stop and pick them up.

I pick up trash.
When people put it out,
I pitch it in this truck.

Who works where you live?
Smile at them.
You will like them!

Think and Share

Talk About It *Who Works Here?* is about workers in a community. Tell about the job that interests you the most.

1. Use the pictures below to summarize what you learned. **Retell**

2. What did the author want you to learn from *Who Works Here?* **Author's Purpose**

3. What questions did you ask yourself as you read? **Ask Questions**

Look Back and Write Look back at page 77. What does this worker do?

Meet the Author

Melissa Blackwell Burke

Melissa Blackwell Burke grew up in a small town in Texas. She loved to visit the library. She says, "When I was a little girl, I wanted to be many things, including a teacher, a newspaper reporter, and a librarian. I have been two of those—a teacher and a newspaper reporter. Who knows—I might still become a librarian some day!"

Read other books about neighborhood workers.

Neighborhood Map

Use this map to check out where people live and work in this busy neighborhood.

- Who works on Pine Lane?

- Who works on Park Drive?

- Where is the bus stop?

- Where can you get stamps?

- Where is the truck that picks up the trash?

White Lane

Elm Drive

Park Drive

Pine Lane

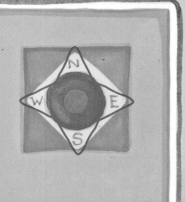

Write Now

Writing and Grammar

Want Ad

Prompt

Who Works Here? tells about some jobs people do. Think about a teacher's job. Now write a want ad for a teacher telling what a teacher does.

Writing Trait

Follow **conventions** when you write sentences.

Student Model

Lyons School needs a first-grade teacher to replace Ms. Parks next year. This teacher must like children and have teaching experience. This teacher must also teach summer school.

Writer names job.

Conventions include capital letter and period for title.

Details tell what teacher does.

82

Grammar

Special Titles

A **title** can come before the name of a person. A title begins with a capital letter. Some titles end with a **period (.)**.

Officer Black helps **Ms.** Timms.
Dr. Ori knows **Mr.** Green.

. . . .

Write two sentences. Tell what a firefighter named Mr. Jones and a vet named Dr. Kraus do in their jobs.

Let's Talk About
Communities in Nature

Words to Read

| there |
| down |
| inside |
| now |
| together |

Read the Words

1. I smell a baby there.

2. T. Rex ran up the slope and down.

3. The small animals went inside the circle.

4. Now T. Rex couldn't get his lunch.

5. They like being together.

Genre: Fiction
Fiction stories are made-up stories. Next you will read a made-up story about dinosaurs that lived a long time ago.

The Big Circle

by Eric Kimmel

illustrated by Richard Bernal

Who lived here long ago?

Big T. Rex wakes up.
Now Big T. Rex wants to eat,
but not bones and not stones.

Big T. Rex wants meat to eat.

Here is a herd of triceratops.
They are going home.

There they can get good grass to munch. The grass at home will make them fat.

Sniff, sniff. "Hmm," said Big T. Rex. "My nose smells a baby there. I'm good at hunting. I'll get that baby. It will make a good lunch."

Big T. Rex rose up on his back legs. He ran up the slope and down. The herd saw T. Rex run up and down.

They had time to make a big circle.
The small animals went inside the
circle. The baby went inside too.

Big T. Rex didn't like this.
Now he couldn't get his lunch.

But T. Rex didn't quit. "I'll make that herd run," he said.

But the herd didn't run.
They kept still in the big circle.

Then they gave T. Rex a poke and a bump. Together they drove him back.

Big T. Rex ran back up the slope and down. Those triceratops saw T. Rex run. Now they are safe.

They are going home to munch grass. Big T. Rex can't get them now. They like being together.

Think and Share

Talk About It The author wrote an exciting story about dinosaurs. Which part of the story did you like best? Why?

1. Use the pictures below to retell the story.
   Retell

2. What happened after the herd of triceratops saw Big T. Rex? **Sequence**

3. As you read the story, did anything confuse you? What did you do? **Fix Up**

Look Back and Write Look back at the selection. Write about how the triceratops protect the baby.

Eric Kimmel

As a boy Eric Kimmel visited the Museum of Natural History in New York City almost every weekend. "The dinosaur skeletons were old friends," he says. "Triceratops and stegosaurus were my favorites."

Richard Bernal

Richard Bernal drew the pictures for this story. "I love dinosaurs," he says. "I have several dinosaur toys in my studio."

Read other books by Eric Kimmel and Richard Bernal.

Class Paper

Ms. Bell and Class Take Trip

Big Bones

Ms. Bell and her class
went on a trip. They saw
bones from a T. Rex.

They saw bones from
a triceratops. There aren't
animals like this now.

Cave Men

The class sat down and saw a film telling of cave men. Cave men went inside caves to live. They went hunting together.

Ms. Bell said, "I'm glad we went on this trip. We'll take many trips like this."

Advice

Prompt

In *The Big Circle,* the dinosaurs work together.

Think about how your family works together to celebrate a holiday.

Now write advice to others about celebrating this holiday.

Writing Trait

Put your ideas in the right **order.**

Student Model

First sentence tells main idea.

Holiday is spelled with capital letters.

Words show the order of events.

The Fourth of July is a fun holiday. You can cook food for a picnic. Then march in a parade. At night, watch fireworks. Enjoy the day.

Grammar

Days, Months, and Holidays

Days of the week, **months** of the year, and **holidays** all begin with capital letters.

The triceratops laid its eggs in **March.**
Mother's Day is next **Sunday.**

· ·

Write a sentence about a holiday you like. Use capital letters correctly.

Let's Talk About
Communities in Nature

Words to Read

grow
food
around
find
water
under

Read the Words

1. The sun helps plants and trees grow.

2. Plants are good food for insects.

3. Birds look around to find insects to eat.

4. Water makes logs damp.

5. Grubs live under rocks and logs.

Life in the Forest

Genre: Expository Nonfiction
Expository nonfiction tells facts about real places. Next you will read about the plants and animals in a forest.

Life in the Forest

by Claire Daniel

What lives in the forest?

We can find life all around the forest.
It is a busy place!

The sun helped
these leaves
grow wide and flat.

Sun shines on the leaves
and helps them grow.
Many bugs like eating leaves.
Yum, yum! The bugs eat and eat.

A woodpecker sits on a branch.
Peck! Peck! Peck!
The woodpecker pecks for bugs.

These holes tell us that a woodpecker has pecked on this tree.

This huge log is soft and damp.
Water has made the log rot.
Small bugs made a home in the log.

This bird hops on the log
and pecks at it. Yum, yum!
It gets bugs from the log.

Nuts grow on trees and then fall all around. Squirrels find the nuts and eat them.

A fox is cute, but it likes to catch small animals like squirrels.

The black bear eats leaves, grass, and nuts. It likes grubs too. Grubs are small bugs under rocks and logs.

This bear looked for grubs under these rocks.

A hummingbird uses its bill to get food from this plant.

Many plants have shapes like tubes. Small hummingbirds like to sip food and water from these plants.

Hummingbirds can catch bugs
for food too.

The forest is filled with life.
Many animals and plants call it home.
It is a busy place!

Think and Share

Talk About It Tell what you learned about the forest that you didn't know before.

1. Use the pictures below to summarize what you learned. **Retell**

2. Why do you think the author wrote *Life in the Forest?* **Author's Purpose**

3. What did you do to get ready to read *Life in the Forest?* How did that help? **Preview**

Look Back and Write Look back at pages 124–125. What do the squirrel and the fox eat?

Meet the Author

Claire Daniel

Claire Daniel learned about forests on a three-month hiking trip with her husband. "That was an amazing experience—being in the forest and living in it."

A bear came to their campsite once. "We heard him coming, so we ran to a shelter. It was a frightening experience! The bear went into our tent and then backed out of it, not finding any food."

Read more books by Claire Daniel.

A Mangrove

Have you watched fish
swim under a tree?

You can find fish in this forest.

These trees grow in salt water.

Fish swim under the trees.

Forest

by Terry Lynk
illustrated by Russell Farrell

Lots of animals live here.

Some live in the water.

Some live out of the water.

They are all around this forest.

Fish find food in the water.
Birds can use fish
and bugs as food.

But some forests like this are being lost. We must save these forests.

Write Now

Writing and Grammar

Report

Prompt

Life in the Forest tells about plants and animals that live in a forest.

Think about plants and animals that might live in a park.

Now write a report about them.

Writing Trait

A report has a serious **voice.**

Student Model

Main idea is stated in first sentence.

Details support main idea.

Many plants and animals live in a park. Flowers and trees grow in a park. Birds, squirrels, and rabbits live in a park.

Writer uses a serious voice.

Grammar

One and More Than One

Many nouns add **-s** to mean more than one.

nut + s = nuts   **bug + s = bugs**

A bear looks for **grubs** under **rocks.**

A bear is looking for more than one grub.
It is looking under more than one rock.

· ·

Look at the report. Write the nouns that
mean more than one. Circle the letter that
makes the nouns mean more than one.

Let's Talk About
Communities in Nature

Words to Read

family

other

also

their

some

new

Read the Words

1. The queen bee rules the bee family.

2. Other bees also live in the hive.

3. These bees do their jobs well.

4. Some bees will make a new hive.

Honey Bees

Genre: Expository Nonfiction

Expository nonfiction tells facts about real people, places, or animals. This article tells about honey bees.

Honey Bees

by Jesús Cervantes

illustrated by Tom Leonard

What happens
inside a bee hive?

The sun shines. The honey bees wake
up. It is time for these insects to work.

Buzz,
buzz,
buzz.

In the hive, bees live together like a family. In the family, there is a queen bee, many worker bees, and some drones.

This is the queen bee.
She rules the hive.

These are the drones.
They help the queen.

Their hive is hidden in a tree.
Worker bees keep this hive safe.

It is not good to make bees mad!
Bees will attack.

Worker bees make wax cells in the hive. These wax cells are small holes.

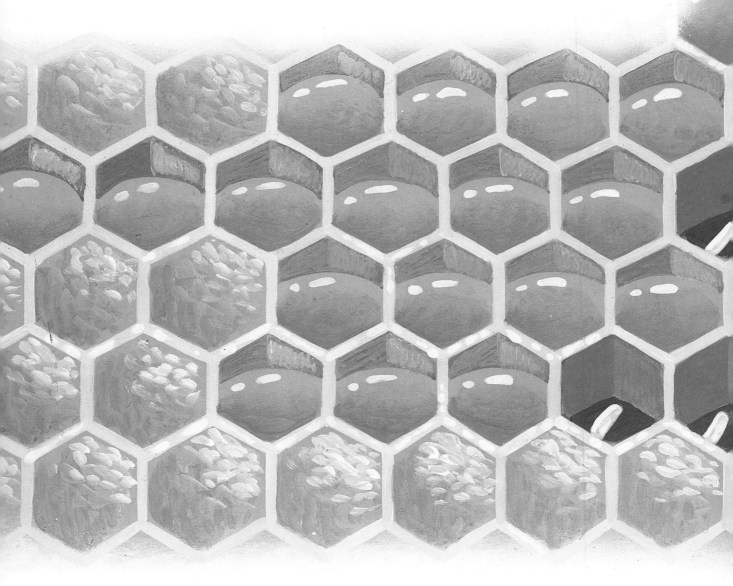

Bees save honey in some wax cells. Little bees live and grow in other cells.

Honey is food for bees.
Worker bees feed honey to
other bees in the hive. Bees
make honey from nectar.

Bees get nectar from flowers.
Honey bees find flowers with sweet
nectar. They take this sweet nectar
back inside their hive.

Worker bees also get
pollen from flowers.

153

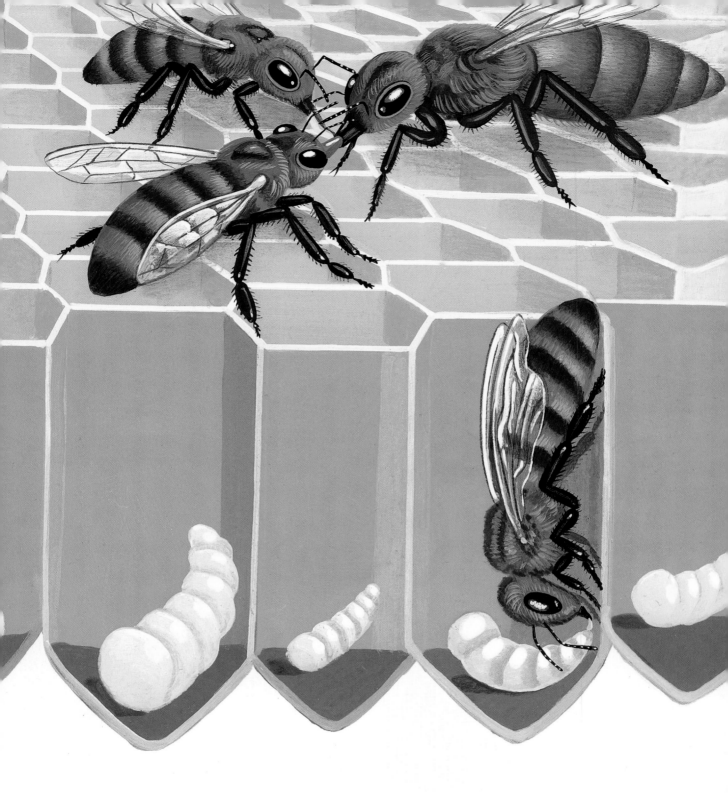

Worker bees feed pollen to
the queen bee and the little bees.
It helps them grow big.

When those little bees get big,
it is time for a new hive.

Worker bees make the new hive.
A new queen will also go with them.

When it gets cold, the bees
will go inside their hive to
sleep and rest. The bees will
wake up when the sun shines.

Think and Share

Talk About It Worker bees are very busy. What do you think is their most important job? Read the part that tells about it.

1. Use the pictures below to tell what you learned about honey bees. **Retell**

2. How are queen bees and worker bees alike and different? **Compare/Contrast**

3. What question did you have about bees before reading? How did that help you? **Preview**

Look Back and Write What kinds of bees live in a hive? Look back at page 146.

Jesús Cervantes

Jesús Cervantes grew up on a lemon and avocado ranch in southern California. He says, "The ranch had lots of bees. They were brought in to pollinate the trees. I wasn't afraid of bees when I was growing up."

Mr. Cervantes thinks bees are great. He says, "I love honey when it's still on the comb."

Read more about bees.

The Ants Go Marching

The ants go marching one by one,
Hurrah, hurrah.
The ants go marching one by one,
Hurrah, hurrah.
The ants go marching one by one,
The little one stops to have some fun.

And they all go marching down,
To the ground,
To get out
Of the rain.
BOOM! BOOM! BOOM! BOOM!

illustrated by Norman Gorbaty

Write Now

Writing and Grammar

Facts

Prompt

Honey Bees tells facts about bees.
Think about what you learned about bees.
Now write three interesting facts about bees.

Writing Trait

Focus all your sentences on one main **idea.**

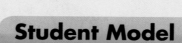
Student Model

Each sentence tells one fact.

Writer uses exact nouns in facts.

Bees live in a hive.

Bees get nectar from flowers.

Bees make honey for food.

Writer focuses on one main idea: bees.

162

Grammar

Nouns in Sentences

A **noun** names a person, place, animal, or thing. A noun can be in more than one place in a sentence.

Their **hive** is hidden in a **tree.**

Both **hive** and **tree** are nouns. **Hive** is in the naming part. **Tree** is in the action part.

• •

Look at the facts about bees. Write the nouns in the sentences.

Wrap-Up

Thanks for the Help

connect to
WRITING

In this unit, you read about many different communities. Think of people in your community who help you every day. Write a thank-you letter to one of these people. Draw a picture of this person.

Dear Mail Carrier,
Thank you for bringing me letters. You do a good job.
Your pal,
Matt

Flower Power

The hummingbirds in *Life in the Forest* and the bees in *Honey Bees* both need flowers. Draw a picture that shows how bees and hummingbirds use flowers. Then write a caption that tells about your picture.

Make a Chart

You have read six stories about communities. Which did you like best? Which did your classmates like? Take a vote. Make a chart with the story titles. Mark a line to show each vote. Give the story with the most votes a star.

Stories	Votes
A Big Fish for Max	III
The Farmer in the Hat	III
Who Works Here?	/I
☆ The Big Circle	IIII
Life in the Forest	II
Honey Bees	III

Pictionary

My Family

mom
mama
mother
mommy

sister
daughter

dad
papa
father
daddy

This is me!

These are my relatives.

son
brother

uncle cousin aunt

baby

grandma
grandmother

grandpa
grandfather

Pictionary

My School

chalkboard

map

chalk

teacher

books

computer

ruler

eraser

pencil

scissors

clock

flag

bulletin board

student

crayon

table

lunchbox

chair

school

playground

cafeteria

classroom

169

Pictionary

Where People Live

houseboat

pueblo

log cabin

mobile home

high-rise

house

apartment building

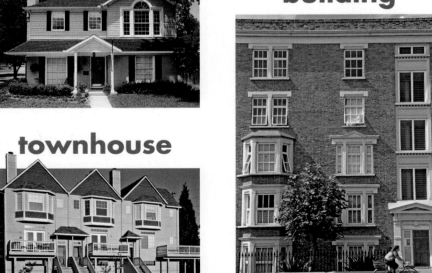

townhouse

Pictionary

Where Animals Live

anthill

nest

hive

cave

den

log

barn

burrow

ocean

lodge

Pictionary

My Town

school

grocery store

bus driver

post office

crossing guard

mail carrier

garbage collector

172

barber shop

library

barber

librarian

cashier

bus stop

fire truck

firefighter

police officer

park

gardener

173

Tested Words

Max and Ruby: A Big Fish for Max

catch
good
no
put
want

Who Works Here?

live
out
people
who
work

The Farmer in the Hat

be
could
horse
old
paper

The Big Circle

down
inside
now
there
together

Life in the Forest

around
find
food
grow
under
water

Honey Bees

also
family
new
other
some
their

175

Acknowledgments

Illustrations

Cover: Daniel Moreton
8, 164 Mark Buehner
11-35 Jody Wheeler
37-63 Pat Cummings
66-77 Tim Spransy
80-81 April Mosakowski Hartmann
85-111 Richard Bernal
132-135 Russell Farrell
138 Amy Vangsgard
140-157, 162-163, 174-175 Tom Leonard
160 Norman Gorbaty
172 Stephen Lewis

Photographs

Every effort has been made to secure permission and provide appropriate credit for photographic material. The publisher deeply regrets any omission and pledges to correct errors called to its attention in subsequent editions.

Unless otherwise acknowledged, all photographs are the property of Scott Foresman, a division of Pearson Education.

Photo locators denoted as follows: Top (T), Center (C), Bottom (B), Left (L), Right (R), Background (Bkgd).

10 ©Gabe Palmer/Corbis
11 (T) ©Tom & Dee Ann McCarthy/Corbis, (BL) ©Sean Justice/Getty Images, (CR) ©Britt Erlanson/Getty Images
36 ©Ariel Skelley/Corbis
37 (TL) ©LWA-Dann Tardif/Corbis, (BL) ©Tom & Dee Ann McCarthy/Corbis, (TR) ©Gabe Palmer/Corbis
57, 58 Wagner Farm, Glenview Park District, Glenview, IL.
60 (CR, CL) ©G K & Vikki Hart/Getty Images
61 ©Melanie Acevedo/FoodPix
64 Getty Images
65 (T) ©Patrick Ward/Corbis, (BL) ©Michael Newman/PhotoEdit
84 ©Stephen Wilkes/Getty Images
85 (T) ©Paul Souders/Getty Images, (BL) ©Stephen Frink/Corbis
113 ©Royalty-Free/Corbis
114 ©Naturfoto Honal/Corbis
115 ©Steve Kaufman/Corbis
116 ©Bill Ross/Corbis

117 (TR) Photowood Inc./Corbis, (TL) Steve Kaufman/Corbis, (CL, BR) ©Royalty-Free/Corbis
118 (C) ©Photowood Inc./Corbis, (BL) ©Tom Uhlman/Visuals Unlimited
119 ©Steve Kaufman/Corbis
120 ©Naturfoto Honal/Corbis
121 ©Fritz Polking/Visuals Unlimited
122 ©Jamie Harron/Papilio/Corbis
124 ©Stephen Dalton/Photo Researchers, Inc.
125 (TR) ©Gerard Fuehrer/Visuals Unlimited, (B) Getty Images
126 ©Jim Clare/Nature Picture Library
127 ©Frederick D. Atwood
128 (Bkgd) ©Bill Ross/Corbis, (BR) ©Royalty-Free/Corbis, (TR) ©Melissa Farlow/Aurora & Quanta Productions, (CL) ©Gary W. Carter/Corbis, (TL) ©Bill Dyer/Photo Researchers, Inc.
129 (TL) ©Stephen Krasemann/Getty Images, (BR) ©Tim Thompson/Corbis
131 ©John Kreis Photography
135 ©Theo Allofs/Danita Delimont, Agent
136 Getty Images
137 ©Stephen Dalton/Photo Researchers, Inc.
138 (BC) ©Ewing Galloway/Index Stock Imagery, (CR) ©Tim Laman/NGS Image Collection
139 (TL) ©Karen Moskowitz/Getty Images, (CC) © Colombini Medeiros, Fabio/Animals Animals/Earth Scenes
168 ©Tim Ridley/DK Images
169 (CR) ©Richard Orton/Index Stock Imagery, (BCR) ©Mary Kate Denny/PhotoEdit, (TR) ©David R. Frazier/Photolibrary, Inc./Alamy Images, (BR) ©Ed Bock/Corbis
170 (TL) ©Jan Butchofsky-Houser/Corbis, (TR) ©E. R. Degginger/Color-Pic, Inc., (BCL) ©Royalty-Free/Corbis, (CC) ©Richard Bickel/Corbis, (BC) ©Kim Sayer/Corbis, (TCL) ©Tony Perrottet/Omni Photo Communications, (BL) Getty Images, (BR) ©John Coletti/DK Images
171 (BR) ©Steve Shott/DK Images, (BL) ©Douglas Peebles/Corbis, (TR) ©Karen Moskowitz/Getty Images, (BC) ©Roger Leo/Index Stock Imagery, (CC) ©Stouffer Productions/Animals Animals/Earth Scenes, (TC) ©Frank Greenaway/Courtesy of the National Prey Centre, Cloucestershire/DK Images, (BCL, TL, CL) Getty Images, (CR) ©Fritz Polking/Visuals Unlimited, (TR) ©Frank Greenaway/DK Images

Glossary

The contents of this glossary have been adapted from *First Dictionary*. Copyright ©2000, Pearson Education, Inc.